READ ALOUD

VIKRAM & BETAL

The Sea Princes

............and other Stories

Retold by
VANEETA VAID

READ ALOUD

VIKRAM & BETAL

The Sea Princes

............and other Stories

Nita Mehta Publications

Corporate Office
3A/3, Asaf Ali Road, New Delhi 110 002
Phone: +91 11 2325 2948, 2325 0091
Telefax: +91 11 2325 0091
E-mail: nitamehta@nitamehta.com
Website: www.nitamehta.com

ISBN 978-81-7676-119-2

First Print 2013

Printed in India at Infinity Advertising Services (P) Ltd, New Delhi

Editorial and Marketing office
E-159, Greater Kailash II, New Delhi 110 048

Typesetting by National Information Technology Academy
3A/3, Asaf Ali Road, New Delhi 110 002

Price: Rs. 145/-

Distributed by :
NITA MEHTA BOOKS
3A/3, Asaf Ali Road, New Delhi - 02

Distribution Centre :
D16/1, Okhla Industrial Area, Phase-I,
New Delhi - 110020
Tel.: 26813199, 26813200
E-mail: nitamehta.mehta@gmail.com

Contributing Writers:
Subhash Mehta
Tanya Mehta

Editorial & Proofreading:
Rajesh
Ramesh

CONTENTS

INTRODUCTION

Just imagine yourself transported back into the time when Kings were brave warriors, undaunted by any challenges presented to them! The collection of stories that we relate in this book originate when a brave king confronts and catches a 'ghost'! This ghost is no ordinary one; to avoid being caught, he actually lays a bet with the King.

He says, "I will tell you stories ending with a riddle, but if you speak in order to answer the riddle, I shall be free to return to my tree!" Spanning from this condition, the reader is treated to a collection of timeless tales, told to King Vikramaditya by the ghost called Betal.

We believe that these tales would impart knowledge and wisdom to children and lead them towards the path of success.

THE GHOST AND THE KING

"Bring the corpse to me. It is hanging on a tree in the forest," commanded a sage to the ruler of the lands, King Vikramaditya.

"Why?" asked King Vikramaditya.

"This corpse is possessed by a clever ghost called Betal. I need to capture Betal. Then there will be happiness in your kingdom," answered the Sage.

King Vikramaditya, soon reached the forest. He saw the corpse hanging on a tree branch. He pulled it down and slung it over his shoulder. Oh no! The corpse, or Betal, immediately lunged up. *He flew back to the tree branch*!

Vikramaditya climbed the tree again. This time he managed to grasp Betal tightly over his shoulders.

As they walked ahead, Betal whispered, "The journey is long. Let me pass our time by telling you entertaining stories!"

King Vikramaditya nodded.

"But if you speak before or after my story, I will be free to return to my tree," warned Betal.

King Vikramaditya readily agreed.

Betal began to relate interesting stories. After each story, he would pose a riddle to Vikramaditya. Sigh! Every time the riddle was asked, Vikramaditya promptly answered! Oh dear, now he should have never answered! If King Vikramaditya spoke, then Betal was free to return to the tree! Again and again King Vikramaditya had to re-capture Betal.

Turn the pages and read the stories Betal told and how King Vikramaditya had to re-capture him many, many times...

THE CLEVER PLAN

Prince Jaikumar was in the forest with his friend, Abhiman, when he first saw the beautiful Princess Meghala. Immediately, Jaikumar fell in love with her.

Prince Jaikumar asked the princess to marry him.

"No, I cannot do that!"

the princess shook her head, adding,

"My father is very strict, he will never agree."

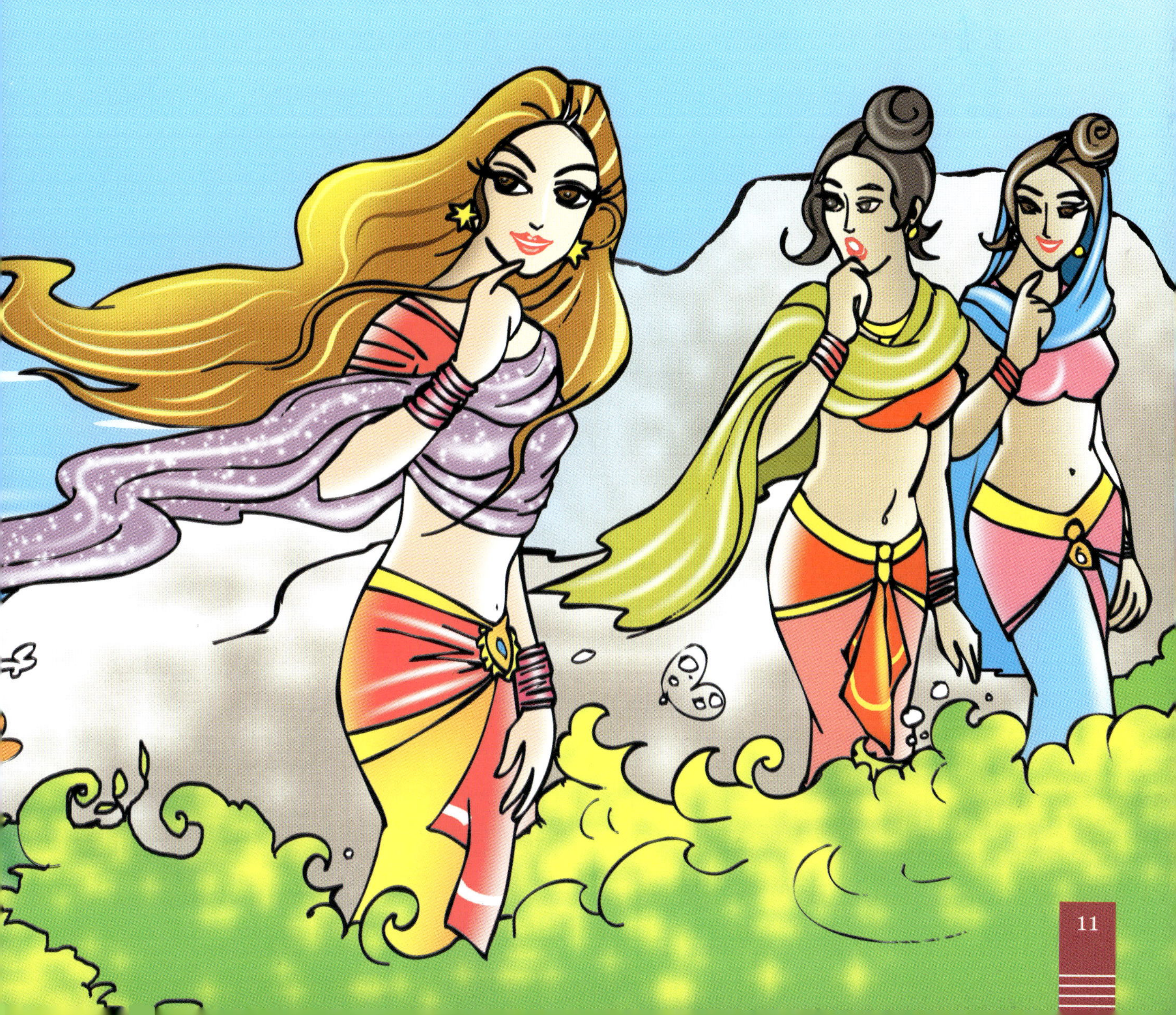

Prince Jaikumar was very sad.

Abhiman, his friend said,

"Do not worry, I have a plan. If it works, the princess will surely marry you."

Abhiman asked Meghala to give him all her jewels.

Abhiman carried her jewels with him and later sold the jewels to a leading jeweler.

Alas! The jeweler recognized the royal jewels. He promptly reported his observation to the royal guards.

When Abhiman was arrested, he screamed, "these jewels were given to me by the princess."

Princess Meghala confessed that she had given Abhiman the jewels. This angered her father, the King, so much that he banished her.

A weeping princess now reached the borders of the kingdom, where Prince Jai was waiting for her. She was overjoyed to see him. Then when he explained that this was all a plan so they could be together, she stopped weeping and she was happy.

Betal paused his story and asked, “King Vikramaditya, tell me who caused Meghala's unhappiness? Abhiman, Jai or her father?”

Vikramaditya blurted, “Her father.”

“Ha-ha-ha-ha you spoke! I get to go back to the tree, ha-ha-ha!”

Yes, since Vikramaditya spoke, Betal was free to go back his tree.

Sigh! King Vikramaditya could do nothing but once again renew his efforts to recapture the ghost.

"Aieee, let me go," Betal screamed. But, Vikramaditya, after a chase, finally managed to recapture the clever ghost.

"All right, since our journey is so long, let me tell you another story. But you know the condition. Before or after my story, if you speak, I shall be free," Betal chattered, hanging over the King's shoulders.

The story...

THE SEA PRINCESS

Minister Jayakumar often stopped his king from sharing his wealth with the poor. His ruler, King Amarnath, was kind and giving. One day, when Jayakumar again reproached the king, the king scolded him and asked him to mind his own business. "I know what I am doing, so please do not keep giving me this advise!" boomed the irritated king.

Angry at this scolding from the king, Jayakumar ran away. He crossed the borders of the realm and reached the sea shore. He sat staring out at the roaring waves. There he came across a beautiful sea maiden sitting on the rocks.

Jayakumar stared at her in fascination.

Seeing him, the maiden called out to Jayakumar.

She said in a pleading voice,

"Please help me find a kind hearted king. Here take this gold and get me the king,"

she again begged Jayakumar.

She handed him a pot full of gold coins! "Please take this and bring me the kindest hearted king!"

"Yes, I know of such a king. Wait! I shall bring him to you!"

Jayakumar rushed back to the kingdom and met his king.

He recounted his experience to King Amarnath, who agreed to accompany him.

Jayakumar immediately brought king Amarnath to the sea Maiden. She was very happy to meet king Amarnath. She knew he was the kindest king. "Will you marry me?" The sea Maiden asked Amarnath.

The king, without hesitation, agreed. The Princess held his hand and within seconds, they were swallowed into the sea.

The king would discover that he was to be the emperor of a large empire below sea level.

Jayakumar was so jealous at the king's good fortune that he killed himself.

Betal paused and asked king Vikramaditya, "Who was responsible for the minister's death?"

Vikramaditya replied, "The minister himself. The good king deserved this happiness. The minister should not have been jealous."

Oh dear! Vikramaditya spoke again!

Betal once again flew back to his tree!

"King Vikram, here is another story," Betal whispered into Vikram's ear as he shifted about on his shoulders. King Vikram had once again captured Betal successfully.

The story...

THE IMPOSSIBLE STATUE

In a far away kingdom, one day, all the sculptors of the realm were asked to sculpt a statue of Princess Shyamlata. However, the King declared that no one was allowed to see the princess. They had to shape the statue to resemble the princess using imagination.

This became very difficult. No one had ever seen the princess! That is why, the sculptors could not make any statue that resembled Shyamlata. The king was very annoyed. He imprisoned them all!

In one of the villages of the kingdom, Vijay, a young sculptor, decided to make this impossible statue! He told his father of his intentions. "I can help you son!" His father then said, "Go to the forest and meet the two witches. They will help you. Tap three times on a tiny stone, which resembles a bull face with horns. The witches will come out."

Vijay went to the forest and found the stone that resembled a bull face with horns. He tapped three times. "Whoosh!" The two witches burst out of the stone.

They agreed to help Vijay. One witch turned herself into princess Shyamlata.

Vijay happily began to carve a statue. He now had no problems, since he knew what the princess looked like.

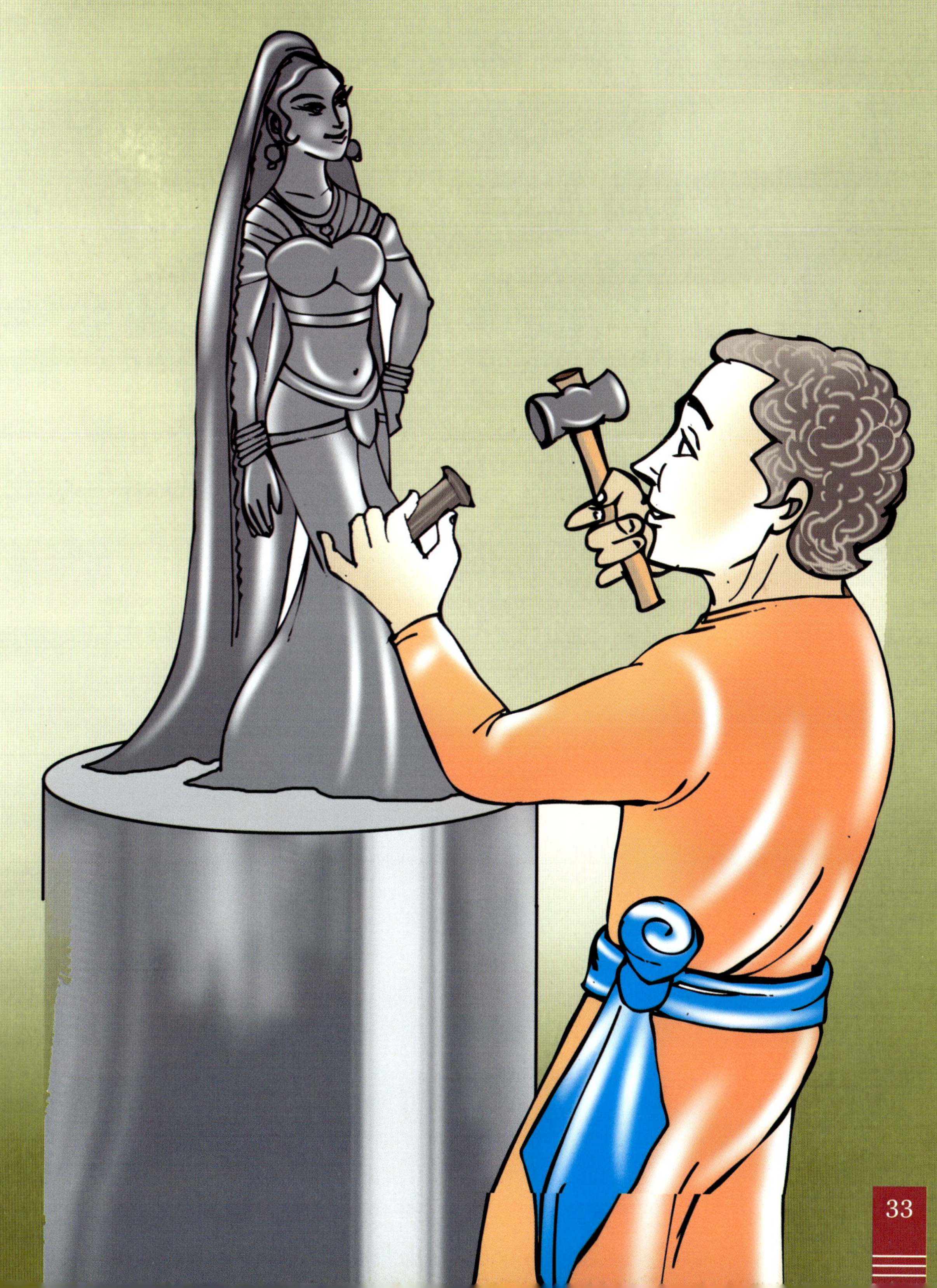

When he showed the king, the finished statue, the king was very happy. But instead of rewarding Vijay, he said, "Now I want you to make a statue of my younger daughter without seeing her."

Vijay did not like this request. He went home and told his father that he had no intentions of listening to the king. That night, Vijay and his father quietly left the kingdom, never to return.

Betal paused and asked a question to King Vikramaditya, "Do you think Vijay was a fool?"

Vikramaditya said, "No, he was not a fool. The king was foolish to think that sculptors could make statues of subjects without seeing them."

Oh dear! Vikramaditya spoke again!

Sigh! Betal ran back to his tree.

THE UNWISE FATHER

This time Vikramaditya held fast to Betal as soon as he caught him. Betal of course could not stop himself from relating a new story.

The story…

One day, a father brought his two blind sons to the court and asked the king to employ them. The king was puzzled that how did the old man expect him to employ his sons who were blind.

The old man said, "My elder son can touch a horse and know its breed and mood. My younger son can feel a precious stone and tell you its quality."

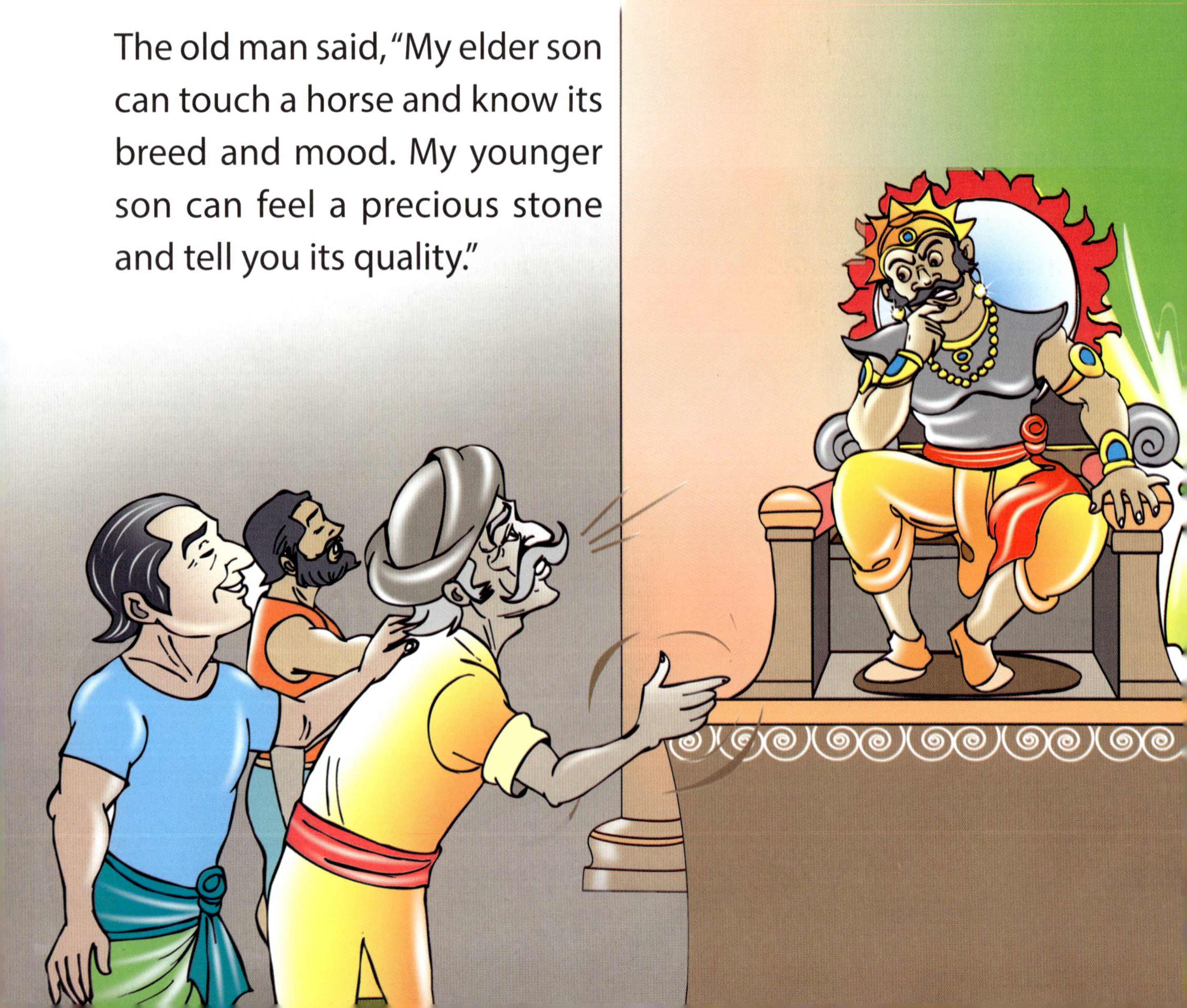

The king decided to test these claims. The older son was taken to a horse at the royal stables. As soon as he touched the horse, he said "This horse is of a high breed, but has a nasty temper."

Just as these words were said, the horse neighed and began kicking viciously. The King was quite impressed.

The second son was asked to touch a diamond that the king was buying from a jeweler. "This is a piece of glass, not a diamond! Do not buy it," said he. He was proved right, when it was discovered that the jeweler was cheating the king.

The old man seeing how overwhelmed the king was, boasted, "I can accurately read and judge any one's character!"

"Tell me my character?" the king demanded. "You are cruel and unkind," said the old man honestly. The King was furious at these words. He immediately ordered the old man to be hanged along with his sons.

Betal paused and asked Vikramaditya, "Who was responsible for this terrible twist of fate? The King or the old man?"

"The old man. The King was cruel and would always be that way. But in his stupidity, the old man spoke the truth and caused his own death and that of his sons," King Vikram replied.

"Wheeeeeeeee!" Betal pushed free. He hovered in a haunting bellow overhead, "King Vikramaditya, your answer is right, but you spoke. I shall return to my tree."

KING VIKRAM MEETS THE SAGE

Once again Betal began telling another story when he was recaptured. However, King Vikramaditya, after some time, did not answer Betal. This way Betal could not return to the tree. Soon they were quickly approaching the forest, where the Sage was waiting.

Betal whispered into his ear, "King Vikram, this time you have won by not opening your mouth to answer my riddle. Take me to the sage by all means, but Vikram, be warned: do not bow in front of that sage! He will kill you if you do so. The sage is a wicked wizard. He needs me so he can achieve his evil intentions. See, as soon as you hand me over, the wicked wizard will dance and chant, then ask you to bow in front of him. When you do that, he will kill you."

"Why will he kill me?" asked king Vikramaditya.

"Because I am actually a very powerful wizard. The Sage will transfer all my powers to himself. To do this he needs to capture me in the form of this corpse," Betal explained in a low voice.

Vikramaditya did not believe Betal. He continued his journey into the forest to meet the Sage.

When the Sage saw king Vikramaditya, he snatched the corpse.

Lighting a fire, the Sage began to dance and chant around Betal and the fire. Then the Sage asked king Vikramaditya to bow in front of him. Vikramaditya looked up and saw the greed on the Sage's face. He remembered what Betal had said. He suddenly realized that the Sage was evil. He asked the Sage to show him how to bow. As soon as the Sage bent to bow, Vikramaditya, with one stroke of his sword, beheaded the Sage. Instantly, Betal woke up.

"Thank you, King Vikramaditya. You have rid the world of a wicked Sage," said Betal gratefully.

Vikramaditya smiled and said, "I have a small request, I would like to repeat and spread these wonderful stories that you have told me, far and wide. May I do so, with your permission?"

Betal gave a big smile and said, "Of course, dear king. Please spread my interesting stories everywhere. With my powers, I will make these tales timeless! Whoever hears them, will gain knowledge, wisdom and success," concluded Betal.

King Vikram did just that and these timeless tales are popular even today.

FIND THE WORDS TAKEN FROM THE BOOK

N	H	E	A	K	V	I	K	R	A	M	N	C	P	A	N
L	R	H	M	C	K	B	E	T	A	L	R	G	H	T	K
E	A	S	A	G	E	E	E	G	H	T	S	M	B	P	W
Y	S	G	B	O	P	S	S	E	A	M	A	I	D	E	N
B	M	A	H	O	R	S	E	H	R	E	G	X	L	W	S

Answer: VIKRAM, BETAL, SAGE, SEAMAIDEN, HORSE

WHICH IS THE ODD ONE OUT?

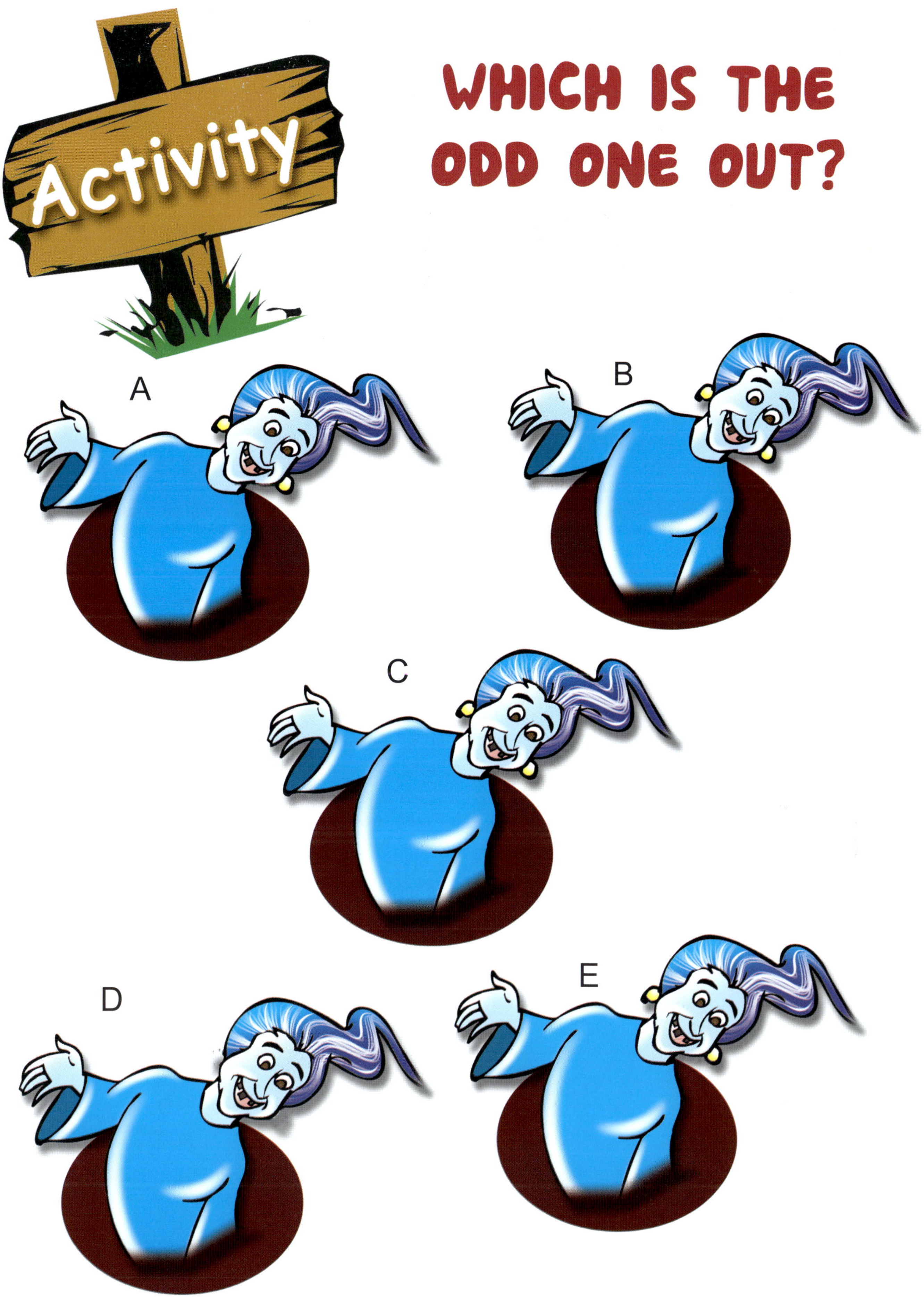

Answer: D (missing ear rings)

Answer: 4